SNAKES

SNAKES

Text by Gun Björk

Illustrations by Ingvar Björk

Translated by Joan Tate

PELHAM BOOKS

Snakes are reptiles. Reptiles usually lay eggs, breathe with lungs, and have skins covered with scales. Reptiles are cold-blooded and their temperature depends on their surroundings.

Snakes are found all over the world, except in the Antarctic.

The **Adder** or **Viper** is a poisonous snake found all over Europe and across Asia.

Head of grass snake

Some adders are grey with black zig-zag markings. These are males. The females are usually grey-brown or red-brown with dark brown markings.

There are all-black adders, too, both males and females. These can be mistaken for black grass snakes, which sometimes lack the usual yellow spots found on the back of the head in grass snakes. Grass snakes are not poisonous.

The adder rarely grows longer than 75cm. Its back and sides are covered with horny scales, and its underside with overlapping scales called ventral plates.

Snakes cannot sweat, so their skin feels dry. The soft forked tongue is used to smell with. The female's tail is slightly shorter and narrows more sharply than the male's.

The underside of the male's tail has pairs of tail plates behind the anus, the opening for its waste matter.

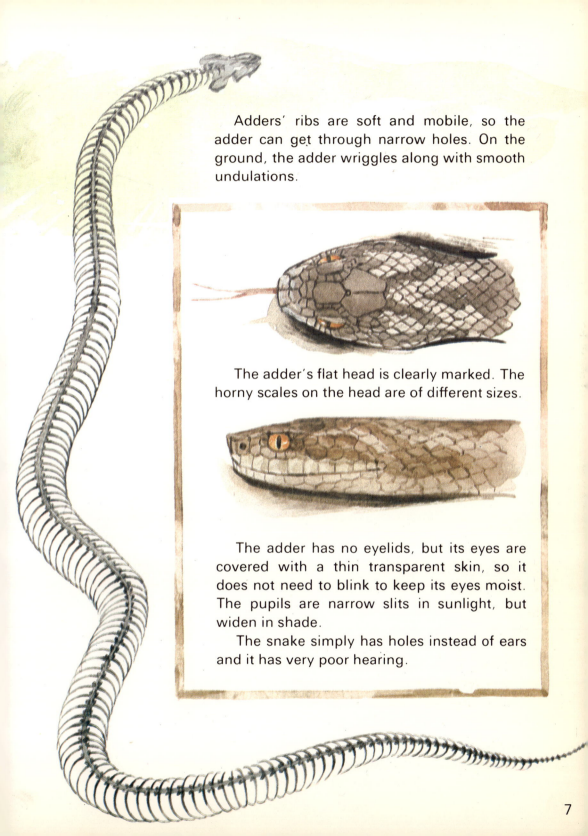

Adders' ribs are soft and mobile, so the adder can get through narrow holes. On the ground, the adder wriggles along with smooth undulations.

The adder's flat head is clearly marked. The horny scales on the head are of different sizes.

The adder has no eyelids, but its eyes are covered with a thin transparent skin, so it does not need to blink to keep its eyes moist. The pupils are narrow slits in sunlight, but widen in shade.

The snake simply has holes instead of ears and it has very poor hearing.

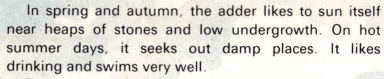

In spring and autumn, the adder likes to sun itself near heaps of stones and low undergrowth. On hot summer days, it seeks out damp places. It likes drinking and swims very well.

The adder is peaceful, but hisses at anyone disturbing it. This is a warning signal and should be respected. The adder bites only for food and to defend itself. If you are bitten, you must see a doctor as soon as possible.

The adder has long poisonous fangs. They are shaped like tubes and are 5 mm long. When not in use, they are folded back in the upper jaw in front of the small jagged teeth.

The fangs drop down when the adder attacks its prey.

The venom, or poison, glands are behind the eyes.
When the adder bites, the venom is pressed through
the tubes into the prey.

9

The adder hunts with the help of its sense of smell and sight. It feeds off lizards, frogs, voles, and sometimes young birds. The adder must first kill its prey by biting it.

The adder lies curled up ready to attack a mouse.

The adder strikes quickly.

Then the adder takes the mouse into its mouth and swallows it whole. It can do this because its jaws are very loosely jointed, so that its mouth can be opened very wide.

The mouse does not die at once – the adder has to track it down with its sense of smell.

Afterwards, the adder rests to digest the food. Then a bulge can be seen in its body for up to two days.

11

In winter, adders hide in holes under heaps of stones and tree-stumps for protection from the cold. When it grows warmer in the spring, they crawl out. They like sunning themselves.

The struggle for the females now starts. The males wind themselves round each other with the fronts of their bodies raised. They try to force their rivals down to the ground, but they never use their poisonous fangs against each other. The winner mates with the female.

The male strokes the female with its tongue and chin. Meanwhile, the female slowly crawls forward. Then she lies still and mating can start. The snakes lie alongside each other. The male has two penises for mating, but uses only the one nearest the female.

The adder grows all its life, so at times its skin becomes too small. Then it has to slough, or change, its skin. The adder does this every spring, while the grass snake usually sloughs its skin later in the summer.

The snake rubs its head against stones and the skin loosens along the jaws. Then the snake wriggles out of the old skin, which rolls off like a stocking. The new skin is very glossy.

If you look very carefully, you may find a sloughed skin. It is paper-thin and brittle. It is always inside-out and is very beautiful.

The adder lives in fields and moorlands and
woodland glades. It can crawl a short way up
rough tree-trunks, and then it uses its belly
scales, or ventral plates, to hook itself on to
the bark.

16

When an adder finds a bird's nest, it often takes the eggs or fledgelings.

The adder is a strong skilful swimmer, but does not like diving, as the grass snake does. It also rides higher in the water than the grass snake when it is swimming.

About sixteen months after mating, in the following August or September, the female adder gives birth to between five and twenty young, that have been inside eggs in her body.

The thin membranes, or skins, round the eggs burst at birth. The young snakes can at once manage on their own, and the female leaves them after a short while. Young adders can use their poisonous fangs from birth.

The new-born adder is only 15-20 cm long and is exactly like an adult adder, except that the zig-zag marking is not so dark. Young female adders are often more red-brown than adults.

New-born adder – actual size

Foxes and stoats prey on adders.

The hedgehog sometimes feeds on snakes, protecting itself by curling up and raising its spines.

New-born snakes are eaten by many different kinds of animals such as toads, crows and
pheasants.

Because of its sharp eyesight the buzzard
can spot the adder from high up in the sky.

When it starts to get cold in the autumn, adders seek out holes under stones and tree-stumps to hibernate in through the winter. They must do this quickly, as they stiffen in the cold.

Toads and lizards often hibernate in snake holes. The adders do not feed during the winter, so do not attack other animals. In spring, the warmth brings them out again.

The **Grass** or **Ringed Snake** is common all over Europe except on some islands and in the far north. It can grow to 120 cms and is thinner and glossier than the adder. It is either black, brown or grey, with yellowish-white spots on its head. These spots are sometimes missing on black grass snakes. Its head is narrow, the pupil of its eye is round with a pale yellow edge, and its tail narrows gradually. The grass snake likes damp places and swims very well. It has no poisonous fangs and feeds off frogs, newts and small fish.

The **Smooth Snake** is found all over central and southern Europe. It has two lines of dark spots down its back and does not often grow longer than 80 cm.

The **Slow-Worm** or **Blindworm** looks like a snake but is really a legless lizard. It grows no longer than 50 cm and has a pale brown shiny skin. It feeds on slugs, snails and worms.

The **Asian** or **Indian Cobra** lives in southern Asia and is about $1\frac{1}{2}$ metres long. It is one of the poisonous cobras. If it is forced to defend itself, it raises its head and expands its front ribs. Its throat then looks like a shield and the spectacles-like marking on the back of its neck can clearly be seen.

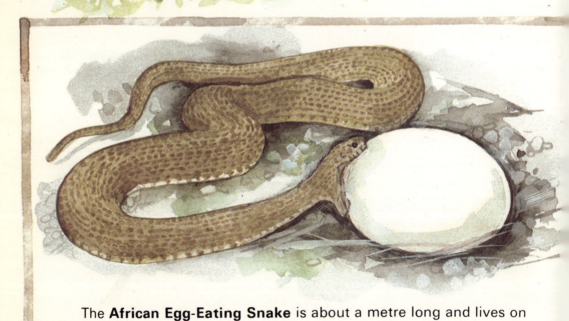

The **African Egg-Eating Snake** is about a metre long and lives on birds' eggs. It grips the egg with its small tack-like teeth. As in other snakes, its jaw can stretch very wide.

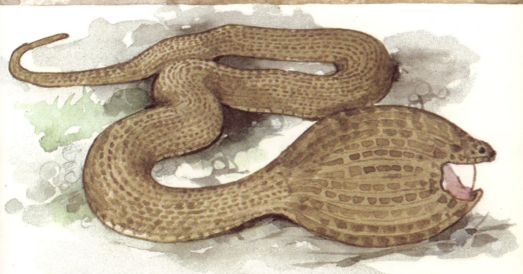

It crushes the shell in its gullet against two spikes that stick out from its neck bones. The contents of the egg goes into the stomach and then the snake spits out the shell.

The **Indonesian Tree Snake** is also found in India. It is very slim and can grow almost two metres long. The snake lives in trees, where it catches lizards and frogs.

The **Anaconda** is a boa-constrictor and is found in South America. It is one of the longest snakes in the world and can grow as long as 9 metres. The anaconda lives in rivers and on the banks of rivers. Among other prey, it catches the capybara, the largest rodent in the world. The anaconda is not a poisonous snake. It squeezes its prey to death and then swallows it whole.

The adder is useful because it lives off mice and voles, so it should not be killed. The adder will live for ten to fifteen years, if allowed to. If shoes and long trousers are worn in forests and moorlands, adder bites are very unlikely. If an adder comes too close to houses and gardens, it can be removed by taking it in a large bucket or a very deep bag.

1   **Slow-worm or blindworm 50 cm**

2   **Adder 75 cm**

3   **Smooth Snake 90 cm**

4   **African Egg-Eating Snake 100 cm (1 metre)**

5   **Grass or Ringed Snake 120 cm**

6   **Asian or Indian Cobra 150 cm (1 $\frac{1}{2}$ metres)**

7   **Indonesian Tree Snake 200 cm (2 metres)**

8   **Anaconda (9 metres)**

Index

Adder 4-24, 30, 31
 anus 6
 bite 8
 colour and markings 5
 ears 7
 eggs 19
 eyes 7
 fangs 8-9, 12
 food 8-11, 17
 habitat (where lives) 5, 8, 16
 head 7
 hearing 7
 hibernate 22-23
 jaws 8, 11
 kinds of 4-5
 length 6, 31
 mating 12-13
 penis 13
 poison glands 9, 19
 predators 20-21
 prey 8-11, 17
 ribs 7
 scales 6
 skin 6, 14-15
 sloughing 14-15
 swimming 8, 17
 tail 6
 tongue 6, 13
 young 19, 21
 venom 8-9
 ventral plates 16
African Egg-Eating Snake 26-27, 31
Anaconda 28-29, 31
Blindworm see Slow-worm
Boa constrictor 28-29
Capybara 28
Cobra 26-27, 31

Grass Snake 5, 24, 31
 colour 5, 24
 eyes 24
 food 24
 habitat (where lives) 24
 head 5, 24
 length 24, 31
 skin 14
 swimming 17
Indonesian Tree Snake 28, 31
Reptiles 4
Ringed Snake see Grass Snake
Slow-worm 25, 31
Smooth Snake 25, 31
Tree Snake see Indonesian Tree Snake
Viper see Adder

First published in Great Britain by
Pelham Books Ltd
44 Bedford Square
London WC1B 3DU
1980

First published as *Ormar*
by Bonniers in Sweden 1980

Text and illustrations Copyright © 1980
Gun and Ingvar Björk

English translation Copyright © 1980
Pelham Books Ltd

ISBN 0 7207 1230 0

Printed in Portugal